The Promiscuity Papers

The Promiscuity Papers

When Sex is No Longer Taboo
A Jungian Analysis of Promiscuity

Matjaž Regovec

The Promiscuity Papers
Copyright © 2011 by Matjaž Regovec
First Edition
ISBN 978-1-926715-38-4 Paperback
ISBN 978-1-926715-39-1 eBook

Published simultaneously in Canada, the United Kingdom, and the United States of America. For information on obtaining permission for use of material from this work, submit a written request to: permissions@fisherkingpress.com

Fisher King Press
PO Box 222321
Carmel, CA 93922
www.fisherkingpress.com
info@fisherkingpress.com
+1-831-238-7799

Cover image © is a painting by Mel Mathews

*A heartfelt thank you to Ann Casement,
Robert Riley, Dale Mathers, Michael Horne,
Erel Shalit and Richard Wainwright for their
support and counsel.*

The Promiscuity Papers[1]

When Sex is no Longer Taboo

Introduction

In this body of work about promiscuity, I will explain how this theme initially found a way into my practice as an analytical psychologist and psychoanalyst. We will explore a few archetypes of promiscuity, namely Chronos (Saturn) and Zeus (Jupiter). In the second part of this publication, we will explore the role of the Oedipus myth in the analysis of promiscuity and I will show how the archetypal theme of promiscuity was expressed in the archetypal transference-countertransference dynamic of an analytic relationship. Finally, I will elaborate on the link between promiscuity and incest.

In 2006, I gave two lectures on the theme of promiscuity. The first was at a psychotherapy conference in Rogla, Slovenia, and the second at another conference in Belgrade, Serbia. At both occasions, I asked the audience what they associated with the term 'promiscuity.' I'd first like to show you the two lists of words:

[1] A proto-version of this publication has been published in "Kairos, Slovenian Journal for Psychotherapy", No. 1/2007.

a) Psychotherapy conference at Rogla, Slovenia

- sexual attraction
- it concerns us all
- to gather experiences
- compulsion
- sex and the love question
- what is the purpose of sex?
- swinging of partners
- separation and choice
- fidelity
- pleasure
- attempt at satisfaction
- suffering
- growing up
- search for security
- the right to choose a partner
- communication
- sex and the question of freedom
- inability to form boundaries
- impoverishment
- addiction
- confusion
- expression of will to power
- inner void
- a substitute
- desire
- lust
- lasciviousness
- search for safe haven

b) Conference in Belgrade, Serbia

- licentiousness
- lewdness
- making it worthless
- atavism
- immoral
- loneliness
- misery
- unholiness
- immaturity
- homeless
- negligent
- directionless

In the responses of both groups, the following psychological terms appear: separation, choice, suffering, inability to form boundaries, as well as confusion, addiction, inner void, search for security, loneliness, unhappiness, misery, immaturity, and unholiness. All these qualities show that promiscuity as a phenomenon is, despite its sexual, i.e. physical dimension, a deep psychological phenomenon.

The Webster dictionary (Webster's Third Dictionary 1993a) defines promiscuity as 1. a) indiscriminate mingling, and b) a brief or random social exchange or relation, and 2. a) promiscuous sexual union. Interestingly enough, the etymology of the word promiscuous comes from the Latin word promiscuus, from pro meaning 'forward' + miscere meaning 'to mix.' Promiscuous could therefore also mean to mix indiscriminately. This reflects what the two groups associated with promiscuity, namely the issue of separation and inability to form boundaries.

Psychoanalytically, separation and boundaries go together. Every separation is a step forward in the development of the ego and personality. Yet, individuality is hard to attain, because promiscuity seems to be a collective problem. Jung says:

> The overwhelming influence of collective emotions spreads into everything... You see this particularly in the American sex problem as it had developed since the war. There is a marked tendency to promiscuity, which shows not only in the frequency of divorces but quite particularly in the *peculiar liberation from sex prejudices* in the younger generation... Promiscuity paralyses... *by offering easy opportunities of escape*... The most recent developments in the field of sexual morality tend toward sexual primitivity, ... where under the influence of collective emotion *all sex taboos instantly disappear.* [italics mine] (Jung 1930, §957-958)

Jung sees the problems in terms of secondary collectivization, as he puts it (Jung 1928, §236). Secondary collectivization is a phenomenon connected with the modern era and with the shifting values that appear at the end of the Piscean age, where old values collapse, but new ones are not yet fully established. Hence the state of confusion and disappearance of sexual taboos. The sexual revolution since the 1960's has seemingly liberalized sexuality and sexual life. Sexual and moral habits which were up until then quite strongly prescribed, as well as proscribed, were suddenly relativized. While I'm aware of some positive effects of this phenomenon, such as for example the proliferation of psychotherapy and counselling in the UK and USA in the sixties, there also developed some difficult issues. Sexuality was supposed to have become a means for modern man and woman's salvation. But what do we get if a taboo disappears? An inner void, connected with a state of confusion and disorientation. In modern psychological terms, the issue of the inner void may be understood as a consequence, or as a result of a lack of object relations. Psychoanalytically speaking, the inner void, which is a recognizable dynamic in the psychology of various addictions, leads us back to the disturbance within the primary mother–child relationship. Hence the word substitute which appears in the list from Rogla. Promiscuity may be seen as an attempt to fill up the inner emptiness, an attempt to find an easy, 'instant,' outer, purely physical substitute to fill this inner void. And so, no psychological work is needed, no therapy, no counselling. No attempt at a possible painful realization is risked. And so there is no growth of awareness and generally, no psychological growth. Promiscuity is an unconscious unsuccessful attempt to circumvent the work that would otherwise be normally done in psychoanalysis and psychotherapy, which is inevitably difficult and sometimes painful.

Such a definition of promiscuity takes us to the necessary and obvious enlargement of the term to other aspects of life. This dynamic may be observed in various other neurotic activities of modern man and woman: for example in obsessive shopping and in destructive eating patterns. In some way, in the modern life of the western world, a psychologically qualitative and rewarding life has been substituted by quantitative and indiscriminate consumption. Instead of inner psychological and spiritual values, there is a quantity of outer material but lack of quality. This is clearly another example of promiscuous activity, being an attempt to fill up the inner emptiness, to find an easy, 'instant,' outer, purely physical substitute to fill this inner void. This means that promiscuity is a larger and more complex problem than some, relatively simple, sexual activity—although Freud with his work suggests that sexual activity is never "simple." However, there exists a reductionist view (inherent in promiscuity), according to which we would tend to see promiscuity as a "simple" phenomenon, where a partner is not a person but merely a vehicle for instantaneous instinctual discharge.[2] Yet, this too is an over simplified evaluation of this problem, and it is precisely this attempt at simplification that seems to be one of the core dimensions of the phenomenon—which is just another sign of how deeply psychological its nature really is.

There is no reference to promiscuity in the General Subject Index of Sigmund Freud's *Standard Edition of his Complete Psychological Works*. However, the neo-freudian Clara Thompson makes an observation:

---

2 See, for example (Bychowski 1959, p. 258), where promiscuity is linked with a result of the inadequate synthetic function of the ego, where "various [developmental] phases and constellations are far from being integrated". Bychowski continues that "this ... seems to be the reason for the incredible ease with which ... so many can substitute one partner for another."

"Adler's description of the possible power uses of sexual activity could conceivably have thrown light on Freud's puzzle about … promiscuity. It will be recalled that Freud felt at a loss to explain … [it] as neurotic manifestation because since libido is being discharged in these conditions, there should, according to his theory, be no neurosis. (Thompson 1950, p. 159)

This takes us back to the old view of the phenomenon of perversion in whose light promiscuity could have been observed, too. For example, Fenichel in his early writings felt that the difference between neurosis and perversion lies in the fact that the symptom is "de-sexualized" in the neuroses, but is a component of infantile sexuality in the perversions; that its discharge is painful in the neuroses but brings genital orgasm in the perversions (Fenichel 1930).

Promiscuity as one of the most characteristic phenomena of our post-modern world has other dimensions and at least the most important ones amongst them ought to be addressed before we venture into the deeper psychological and psychoanalytical issues concerning the psychopathological dimension of the topic. Promiscuous, in terms of sexual behaviour, does not directly and uniformly translate into, and does not equal, pathological. In the second half of the twentieth century promiscuity became more common as is well documented in ethnological and historical literature,[3] as well as in clinical writing. A variety of factors were responsible for this change, including the introduction of safe and available contraception ("the pill"), the influence of the feminist movement on the increased acceptance of sexuality amongst women (women were encouraged to delay childbearing if they wished) and the effects of the gay rights movement in lessening cultural prejudice concerning homosexual sexuality[4] in general.

---

3 Works of Michel Foucault, especially "The History of Sexuality", as well as Dr. Alfred Kinsey's research into sexual behaviour (Kinsey's books were, from a psychological point of view, giving permission for people to experiment sexually more freely), and others, pave the philosophical, as well as practical, pathway to this assertion. For example, Jonathan Ned Katz in concluding thoughts of his work "The Invention of Heterosexuality" summarizes how 'today's meaning of sexuality no longer seems to reside, self-evidently, within our bodies or in nature, but depends on how we use it,' and that 'Americans ... now commonly act as if there's no necessary link between making love and making babies' (Katz, J. N. 2007, p.184).

4 The modern gay liberation movement began after the Stonewall riot in 1969. Under attack came traditional notions of masculine and feminine, as well as the sexual conservatism of the psychiatric professionals. "Promiscuous homosexual" used to be a common offensive expression for somebody who engaged in same-sex activities, particularly in 'sex cruising,' with more than one partner. The perspective now used in clinical practice has changed a lot and has, at least to some extent, succeeded in removing the negative and stigmatizing label of pathologizing promiscuity within homosexual sexuality. For example, Jack Drescher in his "Psychoanalytic Therapy & the Gay Man," shifts our attention from labelling promiscuity as something negative and pathological, to the issue of (non) monogamy in homosexual people, by giving an example: 'one may value enduring monogamous relationships over

Another question which I will attempt to answer at a later point of this paper, is the following: Is promiscuity, defined as indiscriminate mingling, really limited to sexual consummations with many partners, or can it be, in its characteristic psychological dimension, also experienced within a single sexual relationship?

There may exist a biological basis for promiscuous activity. In his essay "Celebrating the Phallus", Warren Colman (Colman 2001, p. 122), quotes Stoller (Stoller 1985: 35) that "from puberty on into adult life, most boys are driven by their erotic physiology more than most girls..." Colman continues:

> "It seems reasonable to assume that a genetically driven imperative to inseminate as many women as possible in order to promote the survival of their own genes is the source of this psychological and emotional imperative in men." (Colman 2001, p. 122)

It would be necessary to complement this research into the promiscuous activity of women as well in

---

non-monogamous ones, even though the latter may also endure for decades' (Drescher, J. 2001, p. 221), as well as his quite realistic finding that 'regrettably, psychoanalysis' countertransferential idealization of monogamy has been inadequately studied' (ibid, p. 288). Drescher, obviously very much aware of the negative connotations which the term promiscuity still evokes, prefers to use the more neutral 'non-monogamous sexual behaviours' instead. The countertransferential idealization of monogamy (which would thus imply pathologizing all promiscuity) is then unconsciously expressed by pejoratively labelling all patient's non-monogamous sexual activity as compulsive, or as a resistance, or as some kind of acting out.

order to counterbalance this finding—a finding that sheds an interesting view on male promiscuity only.

Some Historical Aspects and Turning Points in Society's Attitude towards Promiscuity

Society's attitude towards promiscuity is the result of a long historical development of social and moral values in relation to sexuality. We need at least briefly to examine some important historical aspects and turning points in history that can help us to understand the proliferation of promiscuity in the modern (or post-modern) world. There had been a long historical psycho-social build-up to something that erupted into the sexual revolution of the 1970's. It is at that time called "sexual freedom," but which, as will be analyzed later in this paper, is no freedom at all, but in many aspects rather a state of confusion, where decisions become quite uneasy, difficult, complex and multifaceted.

In the classical world, excessive sexuality *per se* seems not to have been openly tolerated. Although some Great Fathers, as we shall explore in greater detail later on in the next chapter of this paper, were clearly promiscuous, it seems that promiscuity, as with incestuous activity, while it was allowed among gods, was restricted within the world of everyday practical sexuality of mortals. Foucault propounds the classical Greek attitude towards sexual promiscuity while commenting on some important aspects of the love of boys, on which the whole philosophy of love was based:

> By not yielding, not submitting, remaining the strongest, triumphing over suitors and lovers through one's resistance, one's firmness, one's moderation (sōphrosynē) – the young man proves his excellence in the sphere of love relations. (Foucault, 1984, p. 210)

The classical cultural sexual norm regarding the general practice of promiscuity was therefore quite restrictive. It was considered dishonourable to offer one's body to whomsoever it pleased and howsoever one pleased, whether out of weakness, lust, or self-interest. However, this does not mean that promiscuity as such was morally condemned automatically. What seems to have been of utmost importance was honour, chastity and other virtues that determine sound sexual behaviour. It is apparent that much of what we today consider as promiscuous sexual behaviour would not have been either culturally or morally accepted by the Greeks.

A similar attitude is found in classical Roman culture, where it was traditionally believed that excessive sexual activity was weakening and enervating. A man who excessively indulges in sexual behaviour would be considered unmanly—promiscuity would therefore run *contra* to very highly valued and esteemed, as well as socially approved and confirmed, sense of his own basic sexual identity:

> According to the conceptualization of masculinity prevalent in the Roman textual tradition, a real man is in control of his own desires, fears, and passions, and he exercises dominion over others and their bodies. (Williams 1999, p. 153)

"Indiscriminate mingling" would therefore have been out of the question in Ancient Rome, at least if committed openly, that is in the public eye. Society demanded that unrestricted sexual consummation be restricted and limited; this ran in parallel with the imperative of controlling one's passion in a morally firm and effective way. This was in turn reflected in *Stuprum*—the Roman law that punished the violation of the sexual integrity of freeborn Roman citizens of either sex. This would imply that slaves could be used for promiscuous sexual activities and probably they were. Promiscuity, if practiced, was relegated to human contacts within hierarchical relationships. Therefore, promiscuity in ancient Rome was to some extent tolerated, albeit in unequal relationships only. But, promiscuity was accompanied by a strong moral tone, which ran against *virtus*—another expression for the essence of the masculinity of a Roman. Promiscuity ran *contra* to the moderation that was such an important facet of personal moral fortitude and integrity and general social credibility. Excessive lustfulness was clearly condemned as it was supposed to be strictly controlled and not sexually consummated.

The ideals of spiritual love and romanticism of the nineteenth century represent another important historical aspect, as well as a crucial turning point, that needs to be considered in terms of our topic. The romantic ideal put an enormous strain on the practice of human sexuality. True or spiritual love meant that it had to be sufficiently deep and permanent to justify sexual activity. Sexual activity, which came to be perceived exclusively as a consequence and result of such true love, must only be used for procreation, and not on unproductive, libidinous pleasures. All sexuality became divided into normal (serving reproduction) and abnormal (all other sexual practices). Homosexuality as a term was first used in 1869 by Karl Maria Kertbeny, (same-sex sexual activity had no exclusive name up to then), and the term became, after some initial confusion as to what it really meant, condemned as utterly abnormal. Promiscuity fell completely into the cultural shadow of western society. Society's view of sexual *'mingling'* became strictly and exclusively – *'discriminate.'*

Something extraordinary happened with the sexual revolution of the 1970s and 1980s, which suddenly broke the taboo against sexual promiscuity, the psychological consequences of which we do not yet fully grasp or comprehend. For the first time in the history of the western world human sexuality became, at least conceptually, wholly separated from biological reproduction. Although the taboo of sex was suddenly destroyed, a new problem arose. Until then, society held traditional views of male and female sexual roles. People knew what was expected (sexually) from her or him, and knew what to expect (sexually) from others—anything else meant risking the sexual taboo, which could easily have dire consequences. Victorian class standards were clear, offering an illusion of safety and dependability, although inherently repressive and patriarchal. Wilhelm Reich seemed to be aware of this problem as he wrote the following thoughts a few decades before the sexual revolution:

> "The authoritarian familial tie presupposes the inhibition of sensuous sexuality. With-

out exception, all children brought up in a patriarchal society are subject to this sensuous inhibition. No sexual activity, no matter how showy and 'free' it appears to be, can delude the expert as to this deeply rooted inhibition. In fact, it is precisely this *inhibition* of the capacity for orgiastic experience that lies at the bases of many pathological manifestations that occur later in sexual life, such as indiscriminate choice of partners, sexual restlessness, proclivity to pathological extravagances, etc." (Reich 1933, p. 136)

With the sexual revolution came sudden sexual freedom, which implied an exciting opportunity for modern woman and man's salvation—an opportunity arose which undoubtedly contained some projection of a *numinous*[5] kind, and a problem of choice

---

5 In a Jungian sense, it is a known psychodynamic fact that archetypal content can, in certain circumstances, become numinous. The pathological becomes relativized by the numinous. Jungians tend to look behind the pathology, particularly when we come to sexuality. See: "The Idea of the Numinous" (Casement & Tacey 2006). There, in a paper called "Varieties of numinous experience: the Experience of the Sacred in the Therapeutic Process," Lionel Corbett speaks about four main characteristics which he has adopted from William James. Firstly, such experiences are ineffable, and unless one has experienced something like it, one is incompetent to understand it. Secondly, such experiences produce an overwhelming sense of understanding or clarity – they have a noetic or cognitive aspect. Thirdly, the experience is transient, usually less than half an hour, after which point everyday consensual reality supervenes. Fourthly, one's will is in abeyance, in the grip of a superior power, regardless of whether such experience is induced or spontaneous. – It could well be true that promiscuity,

suddenly appeared. Yet, psychologically, choice can only be qualitatively made if we are ready to consciously take responsibility for its consequences. Obviously, one has to work through the new circumstances patiently before any such choice becomes psychologically possible, but the sexual revolution was sudden and irrevocable. This may be viewed as an *enantiadromia*, or turning the situation into its opposite, and is the true reason why we do not yet fully understand the negative consequences of promiscuity, or indiscriminate sexual mingling. The sexual revolution resulted in a state of confusion and conflict, where models from the past were judged as archaic and so no longer relevant. New patterns could only be learned through direct (sexual and psychological) experience. (Post-)Modern promiscuity therefore, beside being a normal reaction to the destruction of sexual taboos and a valid, and at least conceptually accepted, way of western sexual life-style, in its pathological dimension conceals personal confusion and deep psychological conflict of choice in terms of inter-human psychological relationships. It feels as if something is being consumed in its nascent form; it is eaten before it has found space and time to reach maturity. Indeed, one suspects an aspect of collective regression is at work.

---

as an experience of a numinous kind, induces such effects. In addition to this, Jung also says that contact with the numinous may have a healing effect (Jung 1973, p.377). Promiscuity could in this light therefore be seen as a legitimate attempt at "sexual healing".

Secondary Collectivization and Archetypes of Promiscuity

Secondary collectivization or recollectivization appears because of the collapse of the old moral values that were safely embedded within traditional social structure, which contained traditional roles for men and women. In the resulting void and confusion, secondary collectivization sets in, and archetypal forces (being the determinants of the collective unconscious) come powerfully and uncontrollably to the fore. Neumann says:

> "In the course of Western development, the essentially positive process of emancipating the ego and consciousness ... has given rise to an atomized individualism ... there are on the other hand ever larger masses of humanity who have detached themselves from the original situation of the primary group ... to exalt the mass as *a conglomeration of unrelated individuals*."
> [italics mine] (Neumann 1970, p. 436)

In this light, promiscuity as a collective phenomenon could be related to, or even seen as, an expression of mass aggregation. It is a mass of unrelated individuals, behaving according to a newly established collective pattern of sexual practice—a practice that was once primarily for the procreation of the species, yet now seems to serve an entirely different function. Is it merely an additional function or is it a neurotic (or maybe even psychotic) compensation? Or, is it, in its due dimension(s), both?

But of which archetypes are we speaking about? In my research, I have concentrated on the figures of the Great Father, and I am aware that with this choice I have not pursued other possible archetypal aspects of promiscuity. In classical times, the Great Fathers inhabited heavenly abodes, and were thus psychologically safely distanced from everyday reality. These cultures, as we have seen above, made great efforts to develop firm philosophical systems of moral values: moderation, chastity, fortitude, etc.— all of which were of crucial importance in establishing a safe distance from the potentially annihilating archetypal influences of the gods. But, the Great Fathers appear dangerously close to modern man, and certain activities that were once considered to be by permission only of the gods, nowadays have become part of human life and direct experience. Everybody can be a Great Father, just as everybody can be promiscuous in post-modern society!

My question is as follows:

What are the deeper, that is, archetypal roots of promiscuity and what can we learn psychoanalytically from them?

We will analyze two archetypal figures of the Great Father from classical mythology, that of Chronos (Saturn), and Zeus (Jupiter). From there, we will move to Oedipus, for he is a very important Saturnian king. I will show that Oedipus' archetypal aspect of promiscuity, as a variant of Saturnian promiscuity, can only be understood if taken in conjunction with Saturn, and indirectly, with Jupiter. We will see that some aspects of his story are very important and telling in terms of understanding the deeper dynam-

ics of some archetypal transference-countertransference phenomena in the analytic setting between
analysand and analyst.

Saturn, Lust and Denial

Regarding archetypal roots of promiscuity, we find
in classical mythology, Greek Chronos, or Roman
Saturn, the god of time and of the Golden Age. However, Saturn also has a darker face. Despite being
married to his supportive wife Rhea, who is an image of a positive mother, he craves for love affairs,
particularly sexual ones. He is an image of a horny
old man. In his pursuit of the nymph Phillyra, she
changes herself into a mare in order to confuse him.
However, he sees through the deception, transforms
himself into a stallion and mounts her. Out of this
coupling, a centaur Chiron is born, half man, half
horse. Seeing this, Chronos flees, denying all responsibility. Phillyra is ashamed and rejects the child.
Chiron becomes an orphan, and this is his deep psychological wound (although the myth explains this
psychological wound in a concrete way). Chiron re-
jected as an infant, has to deal with a painful inner
sense of inadequacy and emptiness. He exemplifies
the outcome of promiscuous activity. On the one
hand, Chiron is a wise healer, teacher and philoso-
pher, but on the other hand, his father is an emotionally frozen maniac, and his mother ran away out
of shame. Later Chiron is wounded in his thigh by
Hercules and neither the wound nor his pain can be
cured. On the spiritual plane, he was adopted by the
gods Apollo and Artemis, but on the physical plane,

his pain remains unhealed and he remains irreconciled with the cause of his suffering.

Therefore the resolution of Chiron's pain is a spiritual solution. If we try to translate this into psychological language, this means that promiscuity, in its archetypal dimension, is an attempt to solve spiritual emptiness in modern man and woman. Thinking the sexual revolution has given them a sign that 'naked' sexuality means some kind of solution, loosening the chains of old-fashioned sexual morality, modern man and woman would have fallen into promiscuity. While I'm aware that lust could also be seen as a form of love, for example as shown in Vladimir Nabokov's "Lolita," promiscuity opens up some painful psychological issues nevertheless. The pain that is a result of such activity, is, as the image of Chiron aptly shows, incurable. Promiscuity solves nothing except the naked satisfaction of a concrete biological instinct. Thus sexuality loses its sacred, spiritual function, and becomes banal, empty and, as with Chiron produces a painful and incurable wound. Promiscuity is a Saturnian illness, a Saturnian pathology.

The same dynamic appears in pornography:

> One of the main subterfuges to prevent ... connection is again the old dog's concretizing of eros into sexuality, so that even pornography can be said to be ruled by Saturn. Pornographic eros that has no soul in it, differs hardly from the dried, profaned, and loveless psyche of academic psychology, another preserve of the senex. The dry calls up lubricity, denial invites pornography. We create the concretistic psy-

> chopathic age by defining consciousness
> as reality-oriented, forgetting the psychic
> reality is primary and that primary in psy-
> chic reality are the fantasies, feelings, and
> values of eros. (Hillman 2005, p.277)

Pornography can be seen as a purely physical and basic portrayal of sexuality, which in its essence is primarily meant to serve the sacred relationship between two adult individuals. But in pornography, sexuality is devoid of soul. The negative aspect of Saturn emerges and results in the appearance of the inner void.

This therefore is an archetypal dimension of promiscuity for promiscuity is embedded in the root of Saturnian myth. Saturn's sexually manic expression is archetypal. It manifests as a craving for sexual activity that is purely physical, cold, without commitment or emotion that is reduced to the level of merely satisfying a physical desire. In the era of Pisces, it became, through Christian ethos and morality, condemned as satanic (satanic probably coming from the same root as saturnian).

Saturn, or Chronos, in mythology did have a beautiful wife Rhea, but he still lusted after Phillyra. Psychologically, this is a wish to deny and leave the partnership, in order to find a quick, shallower outlet for his or her sexual drive. The relationship with the partner has become too complicated and a question arises—who is going to stay and work on this? Chronos does not want patiently and painstakingly to work on the emotions within the partner relationship with Rhea. As soon as there is a chance, he, as a stallion, jumps out of the relationship and wants quick sexual satisfaction with Phillyra. No doubt his justification would be why wait any longer, if he can, with a little trick and deception get quick satisfaction? But, as soon as Chiron is born, he flees, missing the psychological opportunity of becoming a father and thus losing this opportunity for development. This is another archetypal aspect of promiscuity that it is sex without commitment. In Saturnian promiscuity fatherhood is denied. This is embedded in Saturn's myth which depicts the archetypal conflict between *puer*-senex/father-son and the need to hold the tension between these opposites rather than identifying with one of them. The latter can lead to an over-valuing of the law of the father viz. the tyrannical father versus the under-valuing of paternity or *puer* attitude.

Promiscuity is, in its archetypal Saturnian dimension, an escape from a relationship, especially an escape from the emotional complications, which are otherwise a perfectly normal ingredient of intimacy. Promiscuity is an unsuccessful, and as in the case of Chiron, unendurably painful attempt to appease the existential void of being incarnated in physical flesh.

The positive side of Saturn is the law of the father. This creates a relatively firm and safe social structure that is a prerequisite for general well being. Saturn is the great lawgiver. Yet, on the other hand, he also breaks this same law. With his promiscuous act, he breaks his own laws which he created and which he all the same defends so painstakingly. Hence the archetypal themes of denial and secrecy which are so central to archetypal Saturnian promiscuity. In terms of Saturn, promiscuity could be seen as love that fell into shadow, because it was repressed in order to pre-serve the otherwise positive patriarchal laws of order and morality.

Promiscuity can also be seen as a search for the lost Eden. Saturn's craving for a quick sex-without-ties-consummation of his desire for Phillyra is an attempt at a restoration of the Golden Age. In the mythological Golden Age, which is under the rule of Saturn, there were no conflicts, and all the needs that people may have had were automatically grant-ed. This kills all the possible goals, wishes and as-pirations that people might have needed as part of their psychological development. There is no need to work on anything. Hence, there is no acceptance of responsibility. This creates an absolute calcificatio, or calcination, a complete rigidity. With Saturnian promiscuity, sexuality loses its essential function of human creativity.

The Jupiterian[6] Archetypal Side of Promiscuity

In classical mythology there is a further archetypal aspect of promiscuity. Zeus, the Greek king of the gods, or Jupiter to the Romans, was openly promis-cuous. He not only regularly sexually consummated

---

6 I'm using the term Saturnian instead of "that of Chronos" because it is grammatically easier. However, I'm fully aware that Saturn, being the Roman name for Chronos has in Rome developed an additional dimension as a god of ag-riculture. But essentially, Chronos and Saturn are one and the same archetypal figure. The same mutual relationship goes for Zeus and Jupiter.

his encounters with goddesses, but also with nymphs and mortal boys, girls, men and women. As a result, he sired numerous gods and demi-gods. His wife Hera knew of, but did not condone, Zeus's activities. She was powerless to punish her husband, so in her frequent rages she would attempt to punish Zeus's partners and/or children. The difference between Saturn's promiscuity and Jupiter's was not simply in the frequency of these consummations (Jupiter was extremely active sexually), but also in the nature of promiscuity itself. Whereas Saturn's promiscuity had to be secret, and as such was hidden behind a politically correct social persona, Jupiter's promiscuity was no secret at all. Sometimes it was performed completely openly, almost publicly... The difference lies in the fact that Jupiter generally did not run away from parental responsibility in relation to his numerous children. His main problem seems to be that he could never remain faithful for too long a time. As sure as night follows day he will be chasing the next pretty face that passes by. All his sexual encounters are brief and shallow. This is another type of promiscuity, but archetypal nevertheless.

It is important for Saturn to appear to be faithful to his wife Rhea, and it would be unthinkable to him or anybody in his social circle that he would get divorced from her. His pornographic affair with Phillyra will forever remain secret as he is going to try to retain his status of high social authority at all costs. He will openly deny any possible promiscuous activity. He'll do everything not to compromise his persona and thus remain socially adequate and acceptable.

Jupiter was not sexually faithful towards Hera. She remained his partner, his number one wife, but for sex he usually went elsewhere. He never pretended for too long a time to be a true husband and he never hid his affairs for too long. He had a humorous attitude towards his extramarital activities and was able to make a joke about it. Indeed the word 'joke' itself is derived from the Latin word for Jupiter, that is 'jovial.' This is why Jupiterian promiscuity is more easily forgiven by a patriarchal society, especially because he, unlike Saturn, does seem ultimately to accept some responsibility as a father towards his children. But, on the other hand, it would seem that Jupiter never really takes up real responsibility for his numerous partners and this is a problem inherent in Jupiterian promiscuity. Jupiter represents a new daring order as opposed to the old order of Saturn that was quite well structured and based on realistic boundaries. Jupiterian promiscuity mocks discreetness, thus posing a serious psychological threat to boundaries without which it is impossible to psychologically survive. There is no sense of time and limitation—which are qualities associated with Saturn/Chronos. Jupiterian promiscuity, however liberating and spiritual, brings a dangerously inflated puerile position. The problem of the emotional damage caused to his partners remains unacknowledged. Jupiter has no stomach for emotional complications and turns a deaf ear whenever a partner starts to get angry. If it happens that somebody around him is suffering because of his behaviour, he has little patience. He quickly promises to compensate them, but again it somehow transpires that he fails to do so appropriately.

There is also a serious, difficult and dangerous aspect of Jupiterian promiscuity: Paedophilia. In ancient Greece, it was socially acceptable. In mythology, Zeus was bisexual and he fell in love with the boy Ganymede. In order to be able to have him, he kidnapped Ganymede and took him up to Mount Olympus, the abode of the gods, where the boy worked as a waiter to the gods during the day, but at night, he shared a bed with the "big boss." Here, Hera was automatically excluded, since she was unable to compete in this exclusively male world. Although, observed synchronistically—astrologically, the emergence of paedophilia into the collective consciousness of the world coincided with the entrance of Pluto (being an archetype of shadow) into the Jupiterian sign of Sagittarius (in 1995), it is an archetypal theme. It is ever present. Paedophilia carries with it the obvious psychological disturbance which comes as a result of the abuse of the young person. It brings out a question about the role of ordinary homoerotic playback in the development of masculinity versus perversion. Perversion happens precisely because of Jupiter's inability to acknowledge time and boundaries. Paedophilia is perverse because the sacred purpose of father–child relationship is being abused, i.e. sexually consummated—in this case, in an act of promiscuity. The word perverse stems from a past form of a French verb 'pervertere,' which means to turn the wrong way, destroy or corrupt (Webster's Third Dictionary 1993b). This means that because of the lack of boundaries which forms an archetypal dimension of the Jupiterian new order of things in the father–world, the void in a father–son (as well as in father–daughter) relationship is filled with a promiscuous sexual shortcut, which expresses itself as paedophilia. It is based on inability to form a psychologically developed parental relationship in a Jupiterian social and/or familial environment.

Jan

I will now present two examples demonstrating how these archetypes manifest in everyday life today. The people are real, although I have of course changed their names.

Jan, a man in his twenties, worked as a designer for a well-established older colleague who was an authority in his field. Jan was extraordinarily creative, regularly working on large projects and rapidly being promoted on the hierarchical ladder within the design company.

Jan was gay. His sexual encounters were brief and many. He consulted me because of his acknowledged difficulties in maintaining a sexual relationship. Although he enjoyed sex very much, as soon as there was a chance of developing an emotionally intimate relationship, he became unhappy with the partner, and could even become physically ill, whenever he became close to forming an emotional relationship.

At the time I was unaware of the deeper psychodynamic dimension of promiscuity and I posed a seemingly innocent question: Does the problem lie in promiscuity? Jan did not want to hear my question. He felt offended by my remark, and became angry with me. Jan was sure that he had not yet formed any longer intimate relationship in his life simply because, out of some bad luck, he had not yet found an appropriate partner. He did not want to recognize his inner emptiness. He would rather run away from it.

Jan was very much a *puer* with an insufficient relation to senex. His sexuality seemed to be caught in the sense of timelessness. Only in developing a relationship with senex would he gain a sense of time and limitation. But my interpretation was too direct and therefore offensive to him, and in the moment of the nascent and emerging transference he experienced me as the negative senex. This is something all too common in working analytically with a *puer* who then takes flight. His own unconscious negative senex projection landed onto me and pushed him away, blocking any possibility of my helping him.

Jan craved quick and easy sex. The hunger was simply insatiable. We can understand this as an expression of Saturn, which explains the compulsive character of his sexuality. But, on the other hand, Jan was considered likable and good looking, and he claimed to be easily accepted everywhere, and this energy was frequently consummated in bed with strangers—a Jupiterian element of promiscuity.

After the first consultation, Jan did not get back to me for a few months. He met a new partner, immediately entering into another very intense sexual relationship. But after a few weeks, the story repeated itself—Jan fell ill. But this time, it was Jan's partner who cut off from him coldly—before Jan could do so himself. Jan experienced this as a crossroads. He became aware that it might well have been something within him that was problematic and which could be worked upon. When he told me about this on the telephone, he asked for a list of psychotherapists to choose from, for which I felt relieved. My interpretation from our previous encounter had had an effect on him after all. Time (Chronos) gradually brought the message gently back into consciousness. This time Jan did not run away, but instead a new awareness was born. At times it is indeed a privilege to be an analytical psychologist.

Ines

Ines, a woman in her mid-thirties, had a difficult set of circumstances to deal with in her childhood. Her father, on the border of psychosis, frequently threatened to leave the family. Her mother felt powerless, and even begged Ines, although only a child, to stop her father. Throughout childhood, Ines experienced overwhelming feelings of deep pain, horror and a powerful constant threat of destruction.

Ines entered psychoanalysis after acknowledging a problematic pattern in her relationships. Almost all the relationships were with promiscuous—unavailable—men. On many occasions, Ines felt a sense of being dismembered. Her craving for emotional depth was always sought through sexuality, but this left her not only feeling empty and unfulfilled, but also as if she had been torn into pieces or destroyed.

Ines had the following dream after eighteen months of regular analytic treatment (two sessions weekly):

> I am supposed to get married. Everybody is already arriving, but I still have to put on my wedding dress. I enter my childhood room. But, when I put the dress on, I suddenly realize I do not want to get married. I realize I am supposed to get married to a guy I do not like at all! I jump out of the building, and run towards the car. But in the car sits an ugly man with a woman who is being utterly subservient to him. I force the pair into the boot of the car and drive in panic towards the state border. But, at the border, I have no documents! There is a group of men who want to cross the border without documents. I hope to cross the border with their help.

This dream seems to reflect Ines's family story. In the old couple Ines recognizes her parents, the mother always utterly subservient to a psychologically labile father, who was still very tied-up with his own psychologically ill mother. Because of her instability, the father had never separated from his mother, and in turn was unable to fulfill a husband-wife relationship, let alone that of a father-daughter.

The man whom Ines was supposed to marry in the dream was someone from her real life—a young man with no depth and an arrogant, condescending attitude towards all things feminine, suggesting that Ines could easily re-enact the familial story.

In the dream, Ines was urgently hurrying to seek safety within the male group. Ines recognized this group as her ex-sexual partners. In life, Ines instinctively, because of the difficult psychological circumstances within the family, had tried to run away from the familial story. This is illustrated in the dream by

her packing her parents into the boot of the car—
her unconscious—and entering promiscuous sexual
relations which carried no possibility of emotional
intimacy, and in turn caused her horrific emotional
suffering.

Ines could not understand why she felt such a
deep sexual craving for unavailable men. She explained to me that it was as if she had to help them
somehow! And, her instinct suggested that this could
be accomplished sexually. One way of looking at this
phenomenon would be that the sexual instinct surfaces, because through sexuality, the Oedipal complex is activated. This is a psychological mechanism
that Freud showed as developmentally present in all.
Normally, this is solved when parents have a mutu-
ally stable relationship and a daughter is able to accept the mother as the father's relevant partner. But
Ines, as a result of the mother's powerlessness and
inability to cope, could not do this; hence the urge
to enter into promiscuous triangular relationships
with men. In terms of the inner psychodynamics,
the ego was in an unresolved triangle with the parental figures. Yet, there was another possible interpretation of Ines's psychological situation. By analyzing her mental structure, another perspective of
the patient's psychodynamic situation emerged.

An emotionally weak mother-daughter relationship, combined with a powerful and dangerous
father-complex,[7] in turn threatened to annihilate

---

7 C.G. Jung's association test, which I performed with the
patient at the beginning of the analysis, did not show any
significant chains of complex associations that contained
any direct or clear hints about the father-complex. However, there were two words in the association test that merit

Ines's mental functioning. Because of the threatening father-complex, Ines was in danger of psychotic complications, possibly a psychotic breakdown.

With insufficient ego strength, and the dangerous and threatening void in the relationship with the personal father, as well as an emotionally unsupportive and manipulative mother, who once regularly manipulated Ines to psychologically hold and even contain the psychotic father, indicated that the patient was dangerously close to a psychotic breakdown. The promiscuity present in her intimate relationships could be seen as an indicator that the archetypal aspects of promiscuity were dangerously close. It was the patient's intense lust for sexuality that suggested the theme of archetypal promiscuity. In other words, the whole story may well be, because of the insufficient ego-strength, entirely pre-Oedipal in its genesis, nature and dynamics.

Now, returning to the dream: While we talked about the dream, Ines was suddenly becoming an-

---

special attention. One of them was 'pride,' and the other 'criticize.' With pride the patient associated virtually nothing and clearly a complex was holding, or 'eating away' any possible reaction. Criticize meant 'to attack,' with a relatively long reaction time, but with identical responses in both runnings of the test. Analysis revealed that Ines was constantly and frequently cruelly criticized by the father. She was unable to stand up for herself and developed a feeling that 'she does nothing right,' as well as that 'she knows nothing.' During her analysis she connected this with a relatively negativized image of self-worth and of poor self-value. There is no question of anybody being proud of her, as this was neither expressed by the father in relation to her, nor from herself alone. The powerful father-complex was further indicated by her frequent feelings of being 'walled in,' or 'buried alive.'

gry. At first she could not believe this. With whom was she angry? And then she realized—her father!

This was quite positive, for how could one be angry with someone in such a position of power? It was a promising sign that deep within Ines's psyche, father was being removed from his pedestal. He was no longer a super-ideal untouchable man. Because of the trust being built within our analytical relationship, Ines's father-complex was beginning to transform.

After a year and a half of intense psychotherapy and psychoanalysis, Ines decided to put an end to her promiscuous sexual relations. She subsequently reported feeling a lessening of anxiety, but still felt intense waves of re-occurring pain.

The Onset of the Negative Transference

Our analytical work started with two sessions per week and continued at this frequency for two and a half years—over 200 sessions. The transference mainly consisted of positive feelings of being protected, as well as feelings of trust. However, an idealization had transferred from the father to the analyst, who was also frequently experienced as the all-knowing one. Having not yet found enough space to develop in our relationship, the negative transference was generally not experienced during the first 200 sessions of our work. However, there were some exceptions: each year as the fee for the analysis went up, Ines reacted. But she felt only slightly angry for a short period of time, that was all. Her anger was brief and she quickly returned to a predominantly positive, as well as idolizing position in relation to the double figure of the analyst.

This was a split within the transference. On one hand, I was perceived as the positive father, and on the other, as the all-knowing one. It intrigued me— was there an archetypal parental figure who also represented the all-knowing father figure?

Oedipus and His Promiscuous Archetypal Element

In the earlier part of this paper I mentioned the unresolved Oedipal situation in Ines's life. On looking more closely at this myth, we find that the Oedipus was actually the all-knowing one. He was the one who was able to solve the riddle of the sphinx! His intelligence was legendary. He had an incestuous relationship with his mother Iocaste. It seems that their relationship was very sexual. Iocaste was in her mid-thirties, and Oedipus was probably not much more than eighteen. It was probably whispered about the city more than once that she looked old enough to be his mother. It is therefore clear their relationship was intensely sexual, and it filled Oedipus' void, resulting from having no primary relationship with his mother. And yet the sexual consummation was incestuous albeit unknowingly. This is yet another face of Saturnian promiscuity: Having been abandoned as a baby on a mountain, Oedipus was deprived of any primary relationship. This deprivation was, due to the circumstances, denied and consequently incestuously consummated. True, as a

Saturnian royal figure, Oedipus did not directly swallow his progeny as did the old king Chronos, but all of his four children—Antigone, Polyneices, Eteocles, and Ismene—later perished in unfortunate circumstances.

We have seen in Vladimir Nabokov's "Lolita," as well as in the archetypal image of Saturn, that lust can be experienced as a form of love. Oedipus and Iocaste had no primary relationship, although they are *per definitionem*—child and mother. Instead of a primary relationship, there is a complete void. Indeed, the void is as complete as it can only be in its archetypal dimension. Yet, one could suppose that unconsciously both Oedipus and Iocaste knew this. In order to survive psychologically, being caught in an incestuous sexual relationship, they need to deny this void constantly, over and over again, until the truth finally surfaces.

Seen in this light, it becomes understandable why their relationship in the Greek drama is so uniformly portrayed as intensely sexual. It re-states that their relationship is devoid of human contact, or put in other words, there is no mother-child relationship. In real life, every relationship has an element of a mother-child relationship, for one needs to feel basic trust with each other and a measure of safety. The Oedipus-Iocaste relationship is an extreme and most shocking portrayal of nothingness. The characteristic logic of the mythological language suggests that this void was (or 'is' i.e. 'has to be'—according to the archetypal pattern) consummated—primarily sexually. Void and sexuality together become an archetype that could be called promiscuity. It means to mingle indiscriminately, regardless of relationship.

The very fact that Oedipus and Iocaste are mother and child, only emphasizes this point—it is in this most basic relationship that sex is taboo and denied and this is why the myth uses incest as one of the most powerful symbols for the one relationship which is in all cultures experienced as the most sacred and intimate—that of a mother and child. It is therefore no coincidence that the myth connects these two dimensions. In a promiscuous activity, the partners are brought together 'by chance,' have 'nothing to do with each other,' and it is 'only sex,' where the partner's excitement finds only the unknown other. But, in promiscuity, the partner is not only unknown, but also *indiscriminately anonymous*. In a promiscuous activity, everything is indiscriminate, not just 'mingling.'

Yet sex can be seen as the most concretized, materialized, earthly expression of a human relationship on one hand, and of human psychological relatedness on the other. Practicing "only sex" may result in being blinded like Oedipus, or orphaned like Chiron, for one does not see what one is consummating. We do not know what we re-enact in a promiscuous sexual act. However, there is always a thin line of moralizing and we should not forget that not every sexual activity that involves many partners, is necessarily promiscuous in its psychological dimension. Promiscuity as a particular sexual behaviour in its psychological dimension is linked with a condition of utter emptiness, initially guarded by a taboo of general psychological unawareness of relationship and of psychological relatedness, where relatedness is, in terms of the very elements of the primary relationship, symbolized by the incestuous relationship between Oedipus and Iocaste, the archetypal son-mother pair.[8] Being dominated by his mother figure, he is under the spell of the mother-complex, which determines his fate. This causes his (initially psychological) blindness in which condition he sexually consummates this very sacred relationship. *Thus promiscuity could, in terms of its archetypal dimension or dynamic, be defined as a material (i.e. sexually consummated) concretization of (psychological) incest.* This brings us back to one of my original questions in this paper, namely whether promiscuity, defined as indiscriminate mingling, is really limited to sexual consummations with many partners, or can it be, in its characteristic psychological dimension, also experienced within a single sexual relationship. It becomes clear that it is irrelevant whether promiscuity happens with a single or multiple partners. Viewed from an external perspective, promiscuity as indiscriminate sexual mingling would usually be seen in terms of many partners. But, in its archetypal dimension promiscuity could be seen as a blind sexual consummation of a psychological relationship—a relationship which through a promiscuous sexual act is repressed and denied. In a promiscuous act, one partner does not know the real nature of the other, just as Oedipus and Iocaste did not know (i.e. recognize) each other. When this recognition did

8 Kerényi (Kerényi 1995, p. 7) points to Iocaste as the very source of royal power in Thebes, for in this city royal power corresponds to matrilineal relationships. She achieves a fame that has never been attained by any other queen, mother, or wife of other Greek heroes. In addition, she had to combine these roles *vis-á-vis* one and the same figure of the hero. I would add that the figure of Oedipus was combined as well—into Iocaste's son-lover-king.

finally dawn into the full light of their awareness, their sexual consummation abruptly ceased—which is again indicative of promiscuity, i.e. in the function of indiscriminate mingling.

This theoretical finding is supported by two other pieces of psychological and psychoanalytic research. The first comes from psychiatric research of Wittkower & Cowan (1944). The second is A. Bronson Feldman's (1960) psychoanalytic interpretation of Arthur Schnitzler's play 'Round Dance.' Wittkower & Cowan analyzed a random sample of 200 army soldiers with venereal disease in order to investigate, among other matters, what motives lead them to promiscuity. They found that habitual promiscuity is related to incapacity for deep attachment to any one woman. A profile of a promiscuous man emerged and it was described as follows:

> The individual, who later becomes habitually promiscuous, carries into adult life an excessive load of self-love; in addition, he retains towards his mother an anxious and undue attachment, together with a certain resentment; while towards his father he shows an ill-concealed, or even outspoken hostility. Many promiscuous individuals reject the idea of marriage because, as they say, they prefer their mother's company to that of any other woman; and if they marry, they often only do so after their mother's death... an element of resentment, which is one of the driving forces behind the endless series of their unsatisfying sex affairs. Difficulties arising from this conflict also account for the split between affection and sexuality so commonly found

in promiscuous individuals. (Wittkower &
Cowan 1944, p. 292-293)

In Freud's Vienna, Arthur Schnitzler secured
Freud's unequivocal applause for his penetrating
psychological studies of sexuality in contemporary
Viennese society. Although Freud kept aloof from the
modern poets and painters, he admitted to Schnitzler
in a letter that he envied his 'secret knowledge of the
human heart' (Gay 2006, p. 130). In Feldman's analysis of Schnitzler's 'Round Dance' the link between
promiscuous and incestuous—promiscuity being a
physical manifestation of incestuous—comes even
more clearly to the fore:

> On first thought it might seem that the
> dialogues of the 'Round Dance' were writ-
> ten in support of the ancient notion that
> promiscuous sexuality is of the essence in
> human nature... The dramatist wanted...
> [characters] to stand... without real indi-
> viduality.... The accidental seduction—the
> moment of promiscuity—its superior force
> and its beauty... If the ego cannot get the
> real thing it requires, it might die or go
> mad, but in general it will accept the rea-
> sonable facsimile, and in a pinch the make-
> believe substitute... in protest against the
> concept that they make love mechanically
> and meaninglessly... Alfred... inspires to
> incest... in his blind quest for the mother
> in the servant-girl Marie... His will to plea-
> sure, after all, is not simply an id-drive; it
> is sanctioned by the example of his father,
> we may be sure... Being basically in love
> with his mother, Alfred naturally could
> not tell his respectable Emma how he re-

ally felt about her... he could not be adult with her... Emerging from the fantasy of coupling with his ideal of purity and truth, he discovers himself again by the body of the stranger he married and sense again the need of remoteness from her... since the deliberate promiscuity fostered by the sapience of the species serves both as mask for and bulwark against the sexual selectivity inspired by our incestuous ideals. (Feldman, 1960, p. 24-34)

Returning to the analysis of Oedipus-Iocaste myth, bringing into consciousness the realization of incest creates horrific anxiety. The blindness in Oedipus which was initially unconscious, that is imprisoned in the *prima materia* of promiscuous sexual consummation, breaks painfully and irrevocably into awareness—something that in the myth is portrayed by Oedipus' conscious act of making himself blind. This can be seen as an act of self-mutilation, caused by unendurable and unbearable anxiety that can no longer be either contained nor repressed nor compensated in any form by the shattered personality—as this function was up until then carried by the mechanism of promiscuous (blind, i.e. indiscriminate) manifest sexual activity. Underlying this thesis of mine is the very basic Kleinian premise that consummated sexual act serves in the function of lessening anxiety. Klein says:

... one mode of mastering anxiety is that the ego endeavours to deny, control or get the better of the unconscious by over-emphasizing reality and the external world and all that is tangible, visible and per-

ceptible to consciousness (Klein 1997b, p.
260)... fear of the introjected 'bad' penis is
an incentive to ... continually introjecting
a 'good' one in coitus (Klein 1997a, p. 199)
... the sexual act... is her [the girl's] also
the most powerful method of mastering
anxiety (Klein 1997a, p. 200)... thus the
sexual act always helps the normal person
to master anxiety. (Klein 1997a, p. 201)

It appears in Klein's view that the manifestation
of sexuality, i.e. its consummation, represents a po-
tent mechanism which also greatly helps us to understand the psychological function and meaning of
promiscuity. Klein elaborates something that is of
utmost importance in understanding the neurotic
aspect of promiscuity as well:

The impulsion to relieve the fear of in-
ternal and external dangers by means of
proofs in the external world appears to me
to be an essential factor in repetition compulsion... Not infrequently the woman's
fear of the internalized penis urges her to
test her anxiety-situation again and again,
with the result that she will be under a
constant compulsion to perform the sexual act with her object, or as a variant to
this, to exchange that object for another.
(Klein 1997a, p. 202-203).

The incest between Iocaste and Oedipus is a promiscuous (promiscuous in terms of indiscriminate
mingling) sexual activity that acts as a way of mastering anxiety (holding it in check)—anxiety that is
continuously threatening to erupt with the conscious
realization of the horrifying truth of incest. *Promis-*

cuity thus becomes a physical means, or an overt sexual mechanism to ward off the realization of the incest. As soon as the taboo is lifted—for the true nature of the relationship is revealed—promiscuity loses its function, as sexual mingling is no longer indiscriminate.

Herbert Rosenfeld, reputable Kleinian analyst further elaborates something similar in his discussion of a homosexual patient, who became more and more promiscuous with other men, after he realized that homosexuality (at that time) was prosecuted by English law (Rosenfeld 1949, p. 37-41). Manifest homosexuality, says Rosenfeld, here serves as a defence against paranoia, whereas Freud in his famous Schreber case merely connects paranoia and latent homosexuality (Freud 1911, p.12-85). Rosenfeld's patient for the periods of time when he practiced promiscuous (homo)sexual activity, did not feel persecuted. In the periods of time when these defences broke down, paranoid anxieties became almost too severe. There is a big difference between latent (homo)sexuality (Freud's research) and manifest (homo)sexuality (Rosenfeld's research), for the first one, amongst other important points of essential difference, cannot be promiscuous—for it is not consummated. Without doubt we can conclude that it is promiscuity, or more precisely, the promiscuous manifest sexual activity, which in the described case of Rosenfeld's patient with paranoia, plays the role of a defence, and not merely sexuality, or homosexuality. *This would mean that promiscuity not only lessens and holds in check anxiety, but also plays an important role as a defence against paranoia.* A similar finding is reported and mentioned by Nunberg (Nunberg 1936, p. 18).

The intimate, yet most important link between the promiscuous and incestuous, as shown through the Iocaste-Oedipus myth, needs some further elucidation. Jung considers the symbolic significance of incest:

> Incest symbolizes union with one's own being, it means individuation or becoming a self, and, because this is so vitally important, it exerts an unholy fascination – not, perhaps, as a crude reality, but certainly as a psychic process controlled by the unconscious, a fact well known to anybody who is familiar with psychopathology. (Jung 1946, § 419)

Jung's 'unholy fascination exerted by incest' may provide another clue for understanding the function of promiscuity. In a symbolic sense, the more similar we are, the more incestuous the mutual human relationship. Incest could indeed be seen as a search for similarity (as signified through the symbolic union with one's own being). Promiscuity would therefore represent a means to concretize and make real such a task by way of sexuality—literally materializing it by means of a concrete sexual activity. The incest between mother and son in terms of the alchemical symbolism produces a Hermaphroditus—an anima image (Jung 1946, § 529), which paves a way to the Self. The numinous fascinative quality of the incest (because of its sacred spiritual dimension) is not to be consummated physically—although, it could only be consummated in reality by way of promiscuity, for it is precisely in promiscuity that we are sufficiently blind about the psychological relatedness to another human being. This leads us to the *psycho-pathological dimension of promiscuity*. Yet, it would be completely wrong to assume that promiscuity *per se* or in the whole, respectively, is either incestuous or pathological. The same also holds for homosexuality or any other sexuality. *To sum up the intimate link between incest and promiscuity: it is promiscuity that distinguishes and regulates the threshold between symbolic and literal incest.*

An interesting finding comes from an extrapsychoanalytic research, described by Mark Erickson (Erickson 1993), who summarized evidence that secure bonding during infancy is associated with incest avoidance later in life. Avoidance of sexual intercourse is common among men and women who had lived in prolonged intimacy during childhood. He reviewed studies indicating that sexual avoidance often developed between Israeli men and women who had been raised on a kibbutz together. The same sexual aversion has been observed among Chinese married as children and reared together. Erickson summarizes:

> The adult who bonded securely in childhood should have stable intrapsychic boundaries between sexual and familial feelings... The familial bond hypothesis predicts that any disruption of parent-child bonding patterns contributes to the likelihood of incest. (Erickson 1993, p. 415)

I would like to return to one of my initial assertions about separation, lack of boundaries and inner void that result from an interruption within the primary mother-child relationship. Erickson hear speaks of actual incest—clearly in a promiscuous sexual act between the members of one family, where the familial bond has been severed and in a certain dimension lost and drowned in the unconscious—*here promiscuous in the form of an incestuous sexual consummation fills this void that results from the early disrupted primary relationship.* In other words: Only when early bonding is disrupted is incest likely to occur. Or: Incestuous motivations and fantasies might be evidence of the disruption of early bonding and the psychopathology that results. (Friedman after Erickson 2002) This would support my thesis that promiscuity involves blindness, or an unawareness of the true nature of the relationship. The Iocaste-Oedipus myth is an extreme portrayal of promiscuity actualizing incest, facilitated by a complete absence of any primary relationship between mother and son. The same may hold true for a disruption of the father-daughter relationship:

> ... the timid withdrawal of the father from his growing daughter. The failure of the sublimated relation between the two may deeply injure the girl and cause her resentfully to turn away from her father... prostitution fantasies are mobilized, and promiscuity may result. (Deutsch 1947, p. 265)

Again, promiscuity is linked with the void in a familial relationship, in this case between father and daughter,[9] although Walters (1965) attributed

9 Something similar was found by Kasanin (1940), who reported that promiscuity in women may be manifestations

promiscuity in adolescent girls to a re-enactment of the infantile tie to the mother, yet Kasanin (1940) seems to confirm Deutsch's view. If promiscuity is archetypal, as we see it in the Oedipus-Iocaste myth, then one can realize that this observation of Helene Deutsch matches with the well-known Jungian psychological equation that says that the more developed the human relationship, the less powerful the archetypal relationship, and vice-versa.

The same dynamic of promiscuity could also be seen from another angle:

> ... disillusionment and the incest-prohibition, with all their consequences of secret hostility to husband or wife, will alienate the other partner and drive him or her involuntarily to seek for new love-objects. (Horney 1928, p. 323)

> I find it completely understandable why in my view homosexuality and polygamy stand together on the same side of the equation; fearful phantasies prevent the boy from coming closer to the mother, and they push the boy away from the mother, thus allowing for both polygamy and homosexuality to be encouraged, and both phenomena are therefore an expression of the inability of the boy to come closer to the mother... in these fantasies, the mother's hidden vaginal penis, from which the boy has such a fear, could play

of an acting out process by which the individual discharges energies and tensions resulting from repressed conflicts usually involving the father. In one of these cases the patient developed a psychosis which was interpreted as being due to a weak ego's inability to deal with hostility.

an important role. (Boehm 1920, p. 316, translation mine)

The definition of promiscuity as used in this paper would enable both statements of these two early psychoanalysts to be understood in terms of the dynamics of promiscuity. Promiscuity is a manifest sexual activity with the unknown other:

> We wish to take and be taken with the absolute commitment of the phallic to its goal. The sexual problem of marriage is so often that the phallic excitement is lost from the relationship and excitement finds only the unknown other. (Mendoza 2001, p. 162)

Promiscuity could in this sense be seen as an unconscious search and affirmation of similarity, but it only works as long as we are, in outer terms, excited by the "unknown" other. The search and affirmation of "similarity" could also account for the high frequency of promiscuity in homosexual relations —the fact which nevertheless does not in any way limit promiscuity to be linked particularly with any particular kind of sexual orientation, for promiscuity is well known and documented in heterosexual relationships just as well. However, the sexual taboo that still frequently surrounds homosexuality requires from us that we be aware of our defensive tendency to project promiscuous, which we want to disown as bad, onto the homosexual. Yet, if there exists an archetypal dimension of (male) homosexuality, I suspect it could be in some subtle and inherent way well linked precisely with promiscuity for homosexual promiscuity is in outer (physical) terms (there is no female genitalia) seemingly even further away from the incestuous son-mother pair than a heterosexual relation. There is a general agreement (Willick 1988, p. 435) that there are many different types of homosexuals. However, despite the many differences, promiscuity seems to be the rule rather than the exception, even for many homosexuals engaged in long-term relationships with a single lover.

In terms of object relations, we find an interesting description by Bychowski (1959). In his presentation, analyzing the functioning of the ego of homosexuals (this could be analogously transferred to other sexual relationships as well), he talks about a partial ego regression as a defence reaction of the immature ego to pre-Oedipal as well as Oedipal conflicts. As a result of the inadequate synthetic function of the ego, the various phases and constellations are far from being integrated:

> This, incidentally, seems to be the reason for the incredible ease with which so many ... can substitute one partner for another. *Here the partner is not a person but merely a vehicle for instantaneous instinctual discharge* ... [they] compulsively select transitional objects as the only bridge between the narcissistic ego, isolated in its complete loneliness, and the human environment ... If we assume that in certain individuals the original love-hate objects leave an internalized image (the introject), then it becomes understandable that, under certain conditions, these introjects become externalized, that is, re-projected onto real and actual persons. [italics mine] (Bychowski 1959, p. 258-259).

What the image of Oedipus and Iocaste also con-
veys, is the fact that in the myth (which is not literal
everyday reality) *incestuous becomes actualized through
promiscuous*. Psychologically, this would mean that
one has to be promiscuous in order to deny relatedness, and viewed in this light, promiscuity becomes
a defence against psychological relationship. In the
language of the myth, promiscuity prevents relationship so that the truth of incest does not realize itself.
Through sex, 'complications' are avoided. In the
case of Ines, her urge to enter sexually promiscuous
relationships could be seen as an attempt to ward off
the terrible and realistically dangerous relationship
with the father. It becomes a means, however unsuccessful in the long run, at preventing psychological
incest between her relatively weak ego and the devouring unconscious which would inevitably result
in psychosis.[10]

The connection between Oedipus (the human figure) and Saturn (the godly figure) is as follows. Denial of the void is unmistakably Saturnian. In both
Oedipus and Saturn, fatherhood is denied, and both
are ultimately expelled. Yet in both figures the father
is idealized, and becomes a redeemer. Just as Saturn
castrates his own father Ouranos, Oedipus castrates
his father by killing him. Oedipus is a variant, indeed a human echo of an original drama of fatherly
denial and castration first performed by the godly
duette of father and son.

A parallel can be drawn between the above mentioned Jupiterian archetypal motif of paedophilia

---

10 See Neumann's *Origins and History of Consciousness* (Neumann, 1970) for a detailed description of the dynamics of
the ego's incestuous relationship with the unconscious.

and a corresponding dimension of Oedipus' father Laius, who was known for his love of boys in general, as well as, more specifically, for the boy Chrysippos, whom he, parallel to Jupiter, abducted to be his lover. James Hillman points to an important aspect of the myth, namely to the infanticide that was intended primarily by the father. Thus the erotic bond between father and son is prevented (and repressed) from the very beginning—as well as enforcing the incest taboo between the father and son. Other boys then become the objects of homosexual-paedophilic desire and lust. Hillman rightly says that "[Laius] hears the prohibition against incest as a prohibition against eros," and that "the repressed returns as homos-eros" (Hillman 1995, p. 128). I would add that paederastic promiscuity, as a direct physical (sexual) consummation of the sacred bond between father and son (which is also erotic, for we all are, as Freud (Freud 1922, Freud 1923) has convincingly demonstrated through his research and writing, on the deepest level—bisexual) serves to cover and deny the incestuous dimension of father-son relationship on one hand, as well as the very psychological relationship between the two members of the sacred pair on the other. Promiscuity is again, by materializing an archetypal incestuous phantasy, acting in the function of lessening the anxiety. However, the myth shows this again works only for a while—up to the point, when the real father's son appears and kills him.

*   *   *

Returning to Ines and her father's relationship to his mother. The paternal grandmother was suffering from a difficult psychosis and frequently hallucinated. The father and his mother were psychologically closely bound together, the father having never really separated from her. Even after being married he frequently stayed with his mother—in her part of the house—which was a family run restaurant, inherited from his parents. In Ines's family, the father's aggression had been an ever-present problem. He would frequently beat Ines's younger brother (two years her junior), and was verbally aggressive and abusive to any boy who tried to court Ines during her adolescence, jealously guarding Ines for himself. Otherwise, Ines's father was very intelligent, well-educated, pursued an active interest in ecology and was generally concerned with the various larger problems of the world, qualities he shared with Oedipus the king(Tyrranos).

From throughout her childhood, Ines recalled intense attacks of awe and apprehension. It took the first 200 hours of our work in analysis before she was finally able to connect these dreadful feelings —with the father's pain. These feelings were unconsciously transmitted to her from her father during his psychotic attacks of rage and powerlessness. Ines was the only member of the family who was able to contain this difficult situation, whereas the mother, who had a shallow and emotionally poor relationship with Ines, as well as her brother, normally cut off from these emotionally difficult family situations. Ines was the one who stayed with the father and who even tried to help him in such difficult fits.

Clearly, an altogether inappropriate and difficult task for a young girl.

During our work, Ines realized that she felt walled-in, in the relationship with her father, a feeling she had regularly experienced during her adulthood. For example, in her work with a critically demanding female boss, Ines found it hard to handle criticism and could easily start to feel 'walled-in.'[11] During her childhood, her father's suffering was also her suffering. In our work, Ines gradually realized that during her childhood a powerful feeling had developed—which she succeeded in repressing into her subconscious—that she had no permission to live her own life. Like Antigone, Ines had an Oedipal triumph with the father and she was repeating that triumph again and again with the unavailable men. In terms of transference, she, because of the particular feelings that we shall examine later, frequently experienced guilt. The analyst was split into the positive father on one hand, and the mother on the other, and it was towards her mother that she experienced guilt in her real life because of her feelings towards the father.

The father loved Ines immensely and Ines knew that her younger brother resented this, that her father clearly preferred her. Psychoanalytically, we were dealing with a symbiotic relationship with the father. Hence no separation was possible. Observing Ines's adult relationships with promiscuous men in this light, we can begin to draw a conclusion that these relationships were an (unconscious) attempt (however unsuccessful) to separate from the sym-

---

11 This is her father-complex. See note 7.

biotic relationship with the father. Without a sufficient primary relationship figure, it was impossible to separate from the symbiotic relationship with the parent. But as soon as such a relationship was sexually consummated, as was always the case in her relationships, it was destroyed. Clearly Ines entered psychoanalysis with a good (although entirely unconscious) reason!

The father's enmeshed and psychologically incestuous relationship with his mother, Ines's cold mother, as well as the half-relationships that Ines experienced with her promiscuous partners, all pointed to a diagnosis that, in the deeper psychodynamic sense, we were encountering a version of Antigone. Ines's father was like Oedipus: His psychotic disturbance bound him forever with his psychotic mother, yet at the same time he displayed the exceptional intelligence of the classic unfortunate Saturnian king. Ines, willingly or unwillingly, undertook to guide her father on his journey of suffering throughout childhood. It is always too soon that a child be required to undertake such a task. Although by now, Ines had been living on her own for a few years. Being like Antigone, a true heroine, she had bought an apartment of her own at the time of entering into analysis. Yet, still the separation from father had not yet occurred. This was apparent for a number of reasons, above all was the fear which Ines had succeeded in bringing to light towards the end of our two-and-a-half years of steady analytical work—the fear of intimate relationship.

This finding was, as we shall now see, a crucial turning point in the analysis. This fear was an indicator of the mixed feelings that Ines felt for me. On one hand, I was a positive father, and in this sense she felt very good about our relationship and how the psychological wound from her childhood was being contained and healed. Yet, on the other hand, there was a projection of the all-knowing one. Ines found me to be very intelligent, well-educated, etc, but this all-knowing figure was idolized as the Oedipus archetype. Oedipus, being extremely gifted, and because of the realization that his relationship with Iocaste was incestuous, became psychologically disturbed, and could indeed be very aggressive... In our analytic relationship this was expressed as Ines's fear, which was only partly conscious. It was a fear of coming too close to a certain dimension of her unconscious that could, at least theoretically, come very close to something like the psychotic tissue informing the matrix of Ines's unconscious identity with the father—within the terms of their symbiotic relationship. This was the reason why Ines had, after two and a half years of working uninterruptedly in analysis, demanded that the frequency of analytic work be reduced from two down to one session a week.

This decision was preceded by a dream Ines had while considering the possibility of reducing the frequency of analytic work:

> I'm flying from another town to the town of the analysis. I'm wondering, why am I using the aeroplane, if the distance between these two towns is relatively so small? Initially, the speed of the plane is quite low, and I'm enjoying the clear view of the sky and the landscape with scattered houses down below. But the pilot

then suddenly pushes on very quickly. I
get a bit concerned and wonder whether
we are going to break the sound barrier?
In the dream I notice a discrepancy: the
physical distance is too short for one hour
of such a speedy flight. Well, the aeroplane
then suddenly lands and outside there is a
housewife expecting us and intending to
serve us food in a local restaurant. I realize
my analyst is also with me there on the
plane. The pilot is asking him whether he
is going to get out of the plane, and stay
in this place or not, as the analyst seems to
come from here originally. But the analyst
replies he left the car in the town of the
analysis and for this reason he is not getting out and obviously wants to go on to
the town of the analysis with everybody
else. In the dream I knew this was just an
excuse. The analyst wants to carry on because he cares about me.

Ines associated 'another town' with the town to
which she was about to depart in order to partici-
pate in a meditation workshop. Likewise, the local
restaurant in the dream is familiar to her—it is in
fact a setting from the primary family who ran a
restaurant. Furthermore, from her associations it became clear that the plane signified the analysis, and
the pilot her inner guide. The analyst's excuse is a
well-known theme from her relationships with men.
As regards the housewife working in the restaurant,
Ines felt that she seemed to offer little relationship,
save the food. We may further elaborate on these im-
ages from her dream as follows:

Another town

Throughout the analysis, Ines participated in various workshops on spirituality, as well as shamanism. A reasonable question arises: namely where did the need come from for these various additional healing techniques parallel to psychotherapy and psychoanalysis?

Surely, this was another indicator of the split within Ines's transferential experience of me as her analyst. On the positive side, Ines had been working successfully within the hermetic vessel of our relationship, but the figure of the all-knowing one was indeed too much even for a well-educated psychoanalyst with various additional skills in healing techniques, spirituality, and astrology! Only in part was I able to carry the oedipal projection. Other aspects of the Oedipus archetype needed to be projected elsewhere, outside of the analytic relationship where more suitable conditions for such a projection could be received.

I hold a firm opinion that shamans are, in comparison to meditation and various other diverse forms of spirituality, one of the best possible archetypal ways of mastering and integrating psychotic states, assuming that the personality is strong enough so that one does not literally fall apart in the process. This is impossible to assess before venturing into such activities. Although certainly risky for someone with a family history of psychotic disturbances, Ines had, before entering analysis, already experienced a shamanic workshop, of which she held a positive opinion. She said it had helped her psychologically, at least in some respects.

The Restaurant

The restaurant represented a familiar setting from Ines's childhood. If the woman working in the restaurant was mother, she offered little emotional support. She was only 'serving food.' There was no father in the dream, yet, there was the analyst, and the dream informs us that he originally came from the place of the restaurant.

The Pilot

The pilot, said the dreamer, represented an inner guide. Analytically, he showed the characteristics of an animus figure. Being a guide, he controlled the speed of analysis (the plane was associated with the analysis), he unexpectedly paused to make a break and he also posed an important question to the analyst.

Excuse

The analyst used an excuse in the dream, in order to conceal his real positive emotions for the patient. Excuses are a well-known element from her relationship with emotionally and physically unavailable men. Men who ran away from responsibility, producing excuses instead.

Ines now suggested that she would like to undergo the second part of her shamanic training, and in order to collect the energy, time and money needed for such a venture, she would like to reduce the frequency of our analytic work, so that she could, in practical terms, organize this step.

I felt how difficult it was for Ines to drag this suggestion out of her body. The countertransference I felt in my stomach was an intense fear of not being understood. It was very obvious she was in fear of how I would react to this suggestion. Will I understand her or will I exclusively and jealously guard her within our relationship? In fact, Ines asked me for permission to do this—as if I was the one who could actually grant such a request. This indicated how much Ines still feared the terrible father, from whom, because of his unpredictable and desperate behaviour, she could still not yet separate. Separation remained impossible precisely because of this unpredictability, and this was yet another attempt to escape from the psychotic father.

Interpretation and the Problem of Interpretation in Working with and within Archetypal Transference–Countertransference

Psychoanalysis is still only a "talking cure," as Freud put it. This means that whereas within the boundaries of the analytic relationship it is impossible to practice shamanic rituals, we do have other means in order to stimulate greater and more qualitative awareness. That's the role of psychoanalytic interpretation. Yet, this essential technique always proves to be double-edged and has to be handled with extreme care.

Of course every analysand is free to decide the frequency of her or his work in the analysis. In outer terms, Ines had been in shamanic training for some years now and she wanted to take it further. This was her conscious reason for reducing the frequency of analytic work. However, the previously mentioned splitting that had also found its way into the transference explained the deeper psychodynamic matrix of our (analytic) relationship, indicating that such a decision was, unconsciously, just another attempt to flee from the terrible, psychotic father with whom Ines still maintained, at least to a certain extent, a symbiotic relationship.

If the aeroplane in the dream was the analysis, then it became important why the analyst in the dream refused to get out for a break. One way of looking at it would be that if he got out, he would join the dreamer and her mother and psychologically become equated (meaning simply identified) with the (psychotic) father. Yet, according to the logic of the dream, this would not be 'the direction of the analysis' (represented in the dream with the town of the analysis). Identification with the father would actually be a step back, for the analytic relationship had taken Ines out of the psychotic and dangerous tissue of the relationship with the father, whom she had dreaded throughout her childhood. The stated goal of her journey in analysis was to develop a human relationship—more specifically a lasting and stable partnership. Yet, it would soon become clear why her animus in the dream posed this important question to the analyst—it was a test of relationship and trust.

The aim of the analytic journey was not to become a shaman, although Ines frequently played with the idea that if she did not find a successful partnership in her life, she would become a shamaness instead. This was yet another example of how the previously mentioned splitting manifested.

But the dream lacked lysis, i.e. a solution. This pointed to the present situation in which Ines alone had to decide whether she was going to carry on with her analytic *opus* to its end, or not. The woman in the dream who invited everybody into the restaurant was Ines's mother and in reality the family used to run a restaurant in the house, where they also lived on the upper floor. To finish analysis, or not, did not seem to be a question for the dream. It should also be noted that the mother, unable to cope with the father's psychotic fits, had escaped from the relationship.

Initially, I dared not to interpret Ines's decision to cut down the frequency, while responding to her transference feelings of fear about whether I would allow her to do so or not, with the countertransference response in which her fear was not justified. This was how a positive father would react. But the question of how this would influence the further analytic work and process, for which I was responsible, remained. Being identified with a compliant countertransference, I was not fully aware of what was actually happening, and Ines reduced to one session a week.

The countertransference feeling was extraordinary. I felt as if I should not interpret. There was a distinct feeling that I should not break some kind of taboo. Sometimes it seemed that I was blind, and unable to think properly, and it took some time to realize that this was Oedipus. His psychological situation, being in a promiscuous relationship with Iocaste, did not allow him to break the taboo, unless one really risks upsetting the whole of his inner, psychological balance, as well as the outer, socially so important and influential role of a Saturnian king. I remained in a position, where I unconsciously protected the Oedipus-Antigone transference-countertransference.

Three months later, following intensive work in supervision, I felt compelled to interpret the situation:

Ines: I really think I have done a lot in this analysis.
Analyst: I think you have. But, I wonder, how did you experience cutting down the frequency of our analytic work?
Ines: Fine. And you?
Analyst: Actually, not so good. I miss the second hour in the week. I think you cut down the frequency because it was becoming too much for you emotionally.
Ines: No, on the contrary, since I went down to one session a week, I feel much better. The anxiety is much weaker.
Analyst: The anxiety is weaker, because there is less relationship. By reducing the frequency you ac-

tually run away from the psychotic father. Unconsciously you were getting too close to him, so you felt you should make more distance.

She suddenly felt very anxious and confused, which was exactly how I felt when I first became fully aware of the situation. During our following sessions Ines succeeded in becoming angry with me:

Ines: What you told me the last day I got really angry about!

Analyst: Good.

Ines: I think your interpretation is possibly wrong. Since I cut down the frequency, I feel no more fear for intimate relationship. I had another dream, in which you sit in the house and I do not dare come into it. I'm thinking maybe you should come out yourself, as I was not going to upset you.

Analyst: In the dream, you did not dare to come in where I was?

Ines: Yes.

Analyst: You see, this is just another image of the unconscious fear of relationship. In the same way as in the dream you did not dare to interrupt the father, who was not supposed to be disturbed, because of his difficult psychological situation.

Ines: I'm starting to feel trapped in our relationship.

Analyst: But this is the same as in your relationship with the father.

Ines: I wonder if this is going to take forever, because if the analysis is going to take far too long, I'm not going to be able to have a family of my own, which is my most important wish.

To this I did not reply. This seemed to be the end of the idealizing transference, as the negative feelings had finally found their way into the generally very positive transference. However, the interpretation that finally occurred, had another very positive effect. Ines said that the interpretation gave her a real incentive to think more honestly about why she had really reduced the frequency. After expressing some anger, Ines was finally able to say that she undertook this decision because she had grown fond of me. This was becoming almost too much for her to bear, because of her struggle with the fear of intimate relationship. The idolizing Oedipus transference prevented her from verbalizing these feelings in the sessions, and this is another reason why she cut down the frequency. Thus, the emotional taboo that existed between her and the father, was finally broken.[12] Feelings of fondness and emotional affection were finally free to be invested into the analytic relationship, which up to this point had struggled with the inner emptiness, which stemmed from the relationship with her father and manifested itself in promiscuous relationships in her adult sexual life. At this point, Ines even considered returning to two sessions a week. Yet, this emotional recognition within the analytic relationship proved not to be enough. Shortly afterwards, there suddenly appeared another unexpected dimension of the transference:

Ines: I'm still angry with you for your interpretation.

---

12 I sense this is what Lacan means by the Name-of-the-father—being able to verbalize in the course of analysis what could not be named before which can otherwise lead to psychosis. (Lacan 1958, p. 240). See also note 10.

Analyst: I understand. You could never be angry with your father, because it was too dangerous for you.

Ines: It feels as if you would like to trap me back into my father-complex. I'm considering terminating the analysis.

Analyst: Why do you want to terminate now? Your goals aren't yet achieved.

Ines: On the one hand, you are quite right. I've still got many fears for relationship, it's true. But on the other, I feel you do not recognize that I have travelled so far in the analysis.

Analyst: Is this the plane in the dream?

Ines: Indeed. It takes one hour in the dream, to get there.

Analyst: Does it in any way have to do with you cutting down the frequency to one hour a week?

Ines: Maybe. I think that an hour of analysis with you is extremely expensive, and it ought to take me much further for the amount of money I'm paying for each hour. And the analysis is too slow, and I'm getting impatient. Will I ever get there? Maybe this is why, in the dream, I'm using the aeroplane for a distance so short.

Analyst: How does it feel?

Ines: Angry. Also, I constantly feel that you do not acknowledge how far I travelled and you still think I have unresolved issues with my father.

Analyst: But of course you did a great deal, what do you mean?

Ines: Ok. It is alright emotionally. A few days ago, I was even able to go to my father, embrace him and tell him how much I care for him. This was for the first time in my life I did such a thing!

Analyst: Oh, this is really important. How did it feel?

Ines: Very good. He also showed me he was moved, and it was most important you showed to me that you cared for me and that you missed our second hour in the week. This opened up my heart, and I generally feel so much better emotionally now, in general.

Analyst: So what's coming up?

Ines: It's... gosh! Something I didn't dare to bring up until now, and it's been around for such a long time. It's a persistent dream that you are trying to approach me sexually in our sessions. I didn't dare to say anything about it, as it was too embarrassing.

Analyst: I understand.

This is the final breaking of the sexual taboo. The archetypal sexual transference was released and I suddenly understood where my persistent feelings of taboo came from during the past years of working with Ines. Analysis finally revealed the archetypal transference-countertransference situation, in which the sexually promiscuous myth was working beneath our conscious analytic relationship.

The dream was in its own way heralding this—the speeding up of the plane also meant the realization of the archetypal transference, the sound barrier equaled sexual taboo. The breaking of the sound barrier was then the breaking of the sexual taboo within the analytic relationship and the sound obviously was uttered in the end—as Ines finally did break the taboo by producing the 'sound'—pronouncing it aloud. The dream had left this solution uncertain and open, as dreams often do. Dreams do not decide what the outcome will be, and it seems that at the time of this dream, the outcome was still undetermined. I had to refuse, so to speak, within Ines's unconscious, to be identified with the father any longer (in the dream I refused to get out of the plane)—an act that Ines interpreted as a clear statement that I did care for her. Again, it became conscious at the moment when I told her I do miss our second session in the week. This made it possible to break the barrier of the archetypal Oedipal promiscuous situation that was hindering further analysis and finally enabled the beginning of analytic resolution of the father-complex.

Concluding Summation

In the fields of psychoanalysis and analytical psychology, Saturn and Jupiter are key archetypal figures, and like all keys,** a proper understanding of their roles unlocks the doors which will facilitate a greater understanding of the issues of promiscuity in theory and practice.

Additionally, the Saturnian dimension of promiscuity, as we have seen, does not only imply the dynamics of Chronos (or Saturn) himself, but can be equally observed in the psychodynamics of some Saturnian kings, such as Oedipus. Oedipus and Antigone seem to be especially important figures which enhance the deeper psychological and psychodynamic understanding of promiscuity. Promiscuity, when expressed as intense sexual feelings in a transference-countertransference situation, may be found in the very core of the Oedipus myth. Yet, in the practical analytic work, the road to naming it properly can be so long exactly because the Oedipus' way is so long and desperate. Being the all-knowing one, successfully prevents him from discovering his own incestuous nature, which is portrayed symbolically not by his blindness, which could be seen as an attempt to turn inwards, but rather with his promiscuous relationship with Iocaste. It is not the incest itself, but rather the promiscuous relationship that poses a special psychological problem that I have analyzed in this paper, for the incestuous becomes actualized through the promiscuous. Promiscuity can be an attempt at warding off the psychological incest of a relatively weak ego with the devouring unconscious which would otherwise result in psychosis. Promiscuity only works as long as we are, in outer terms, excited by the "unknown" other. It is promiscuity that distinguishes and regulates the threshold between symbolic and literal incest. Promiscuity is a manifest sexual activity with the unknown other. In addition to this, promiscuity can also be considered as a defence against paranoia, as shown by psychoanalysts like Rosenfeld and Nunberg.

Whilst it would be completely wrong to assume that promiscuity on the whole, i.e. the phenomenon of promiscuity as such, is either incestuous or pathological *per se,* promiscuity as a particular sexual behaviour in its psychological dimension touches on an inner void, initially covered by a taboo of general psychological unawareness of relationship and psychological relatedness, where (un)relatedness is symbolized by the incestuous relationship between Oedipus and Iocaste. It has to do with a certain psychological blindness, which, after the incestuous nature of the relationship is revealed and anxiety, no longer held in check, turns itself into the physical blindness of the suffering Oedipus. Thus the intimate, yet very important link between promiscuity and incest relates to promiscuity as a manifest realization of an incestuous relationship in the service of the numinous fascinative quality of the incest (because of the sacred spiritual dimension of the incest). Whilst incest is not to be consummated physically (something that is prevented by way of the taboo against incest)—in reality incest can *only* be consummated by way of promiscuity, for it is precisely in promiscuity that we are blind to the psychological relatedness in relation to another human being. This leads us to the psychopathological dimension of promiscuity.

**Jung saw astrology as one of the original tools that helped to facilitate spiritual and psychological understanding of the pre-modern world of the Western world. Serious study of astrology was used in conjunction with alchemy, and both of them Jung used to draw some basic premises and foundations for his work which came to be known as analytical psychology. In a private conversation with his daughter Frau Hélène Hörni in 2001 I learned that her father used to calculate, draw and analyze astrological charts for every patient – and that he was doing this during a period of several years. In Ines's birth chart, we find that Saturn sits on midheaven (Medium Coeli), which is one of the most characteristic symbolic parental points in the astrological chart. Venus, symbolizing Eros and erotic life, is found in the Saturnian sign of Capricorn (Capricorn is ruled by Saturn), plus in an important astrological aspect with Saturn (120°, which is called trine aspect and is known for its symbolics of unawareness and conflictlesness – which explains why Ines was so unaware of the difficult Saturnian situation with her real father: in the core of her father image there stands a powerful Saturnian archetypal father-image) in the fifth house – which is the house of love, romance, and love affairs. The latter explains why she had to work for such a long time through a series of promiscuous love relationships with unavailable men. In the astrological chart of Jan, whose sexuality is caught in the Jupiterian dimension of timelessness, his Jupiter is on the descendent (which is the most important point in terms of relationships), making an opposition to his Venus on the ascendant, whereas Saturn sits in the eighth house (which is traditionally the field of sexuality) – something that explains his dynamics of craving for quick and easy sex. Once again, Jupiter and Saturn prove to be important archetypal keys that can facilitate opening the doors of greater understanding and it was precisely with their help (this time in their symbolically-astrological dimension) that I came to be inspired to start thinking about my patients, as well as about promiscuity itself, in a creative and radically new way.

REFERENCES

Boehm, F. (1920): Beiträge zur Psychologie der Homosexualität. *Internationale Zeitschrift für Psychoanalyse*, VIII/3.

Bychowski, G. (1959). The Ego and the Object of the Homosexual. *International Journal of Psychoanalysis*, 42, 1961.

Casement, A., Tacey, D. (2006). *The Idea of the Numinous, Contemporary Jungian and Psychoanalytic Perspectives*. East Sussex: Routledge.

Colman, W. (2001). Celebrating the Phallus. In: *Sexuality, Psychoanalytic Perspectives*, ed. Harding, C. New York: Brunner-Routledge.

Deutsch , H. (1947). *The Psychology of Women, a Psychoanalytic Interpretation, Vol. 1: Girlhood*. London: Research Books Ltd.

Drescher, J. (2001). *Psychoanalytic Therapy & the Gay Man*. New Jersey: The Analytic Press.

Erickson, M. T. (1993). Rethinking Oedipus: An Evolutionary Perspective of Incest Avoidance. *American Journal of Psychiatry*, 150: 411-416.

Feldman, A. B. (1960). The Pattern of Promiscuity Seen in Schnitzler's 'Round Dance.' *Psychoanalysis and the Psychoanalytic Review, 47*.

Fenichel, O. (1930). The Pregenital Antecedents of the Oedipus Complex. In: Collected *Papers, 1*. New York: W. W. Norton, 1953.

Foucault, M. (1984). *The Use of Pleasure, the History of Sexuality: 2*. London: Penguin Books, 1992.

Freud, S. (1911). Psycho-Analytic Notes on an Autobiographical Account of a Case of Paranoia (Dementia Paranoides). In: *The Standard Edition of the Complete Works of Sigmund Freud*, vol. XII. Norton, New York, 1953.

Freud, S. (1922). Some Neurotic Mechanisms in Jealousy, Paranoia and Homosexuality. In: *The Standard Edition of the Complete Works of Sigmund Freud*, vol. XVIII. Norton, New York, 1953.

Freud, S. (1923). The Ego and the Id. In: *The Standard Edition of the Complete Works of Sigmund Freud*, vol. XIX. Norton, New York, 1953.

Friedman, R. C. (2002): Freud, Oedipus, and Homosexuality. In: *Sexual Orientation & Psychodynamic Psychotherapy, Sexual Science and Clinical Practice*, eds. Friedman & Downey. New York, West Sussex: Columbia University Press.

Gay, Peter (2006). *Freud, A Life for Our Time*. London: MAX.

Hillman, J. (1995). Oedipus Revisited. In: *Oedipus variations*. Woodstock: Spring Publications.

Hillman, J. (2005). Negative Senex and a Renaissance Solution. In: *Puer Papers*, Dallas Texas: Spring Publications.

Horney, K. (1928): The Problem of the Monogamous Ideal. International *Journal of Psychoanalysis*, vol. IX.

Jung, C.G. (1928). The Relation Between the Ego and the Unconscious. In: *Two Essays on Analytical Psychology* (CW7).

Jung, C.G. (1930). The Complications of American Psychology. In: *Civilization in Transition* (CW 10).

Jung, C.G. (1946). The Psychology of Transference. In: *The Practice of Psychotherapy* (CW 16).

Jung, C.G. (1973). *Letters*, vol. 1, ed. G. Adler and A. Jaffé, trans R. F. C. Hull, Princeton. NJ: Princeton University Press.

Kasanin, J. (1940). Neurotic 'Acting Out' as a Basis for Sexual Promiscuity. *Psychoanalytic Reviews, 31*.

Katz, J. N. (2007). *The Invention of Heterosexuality*. Chicago: The University of Chicago Press.

Kerényi, K. (1995). Oedipus: Two Essays. In: *Oedipus variations*. Woodstock: Spring Publications.

Klein, M. (1997a). The Effects of Early Anxiety-Situations in the Development of the Girl. In: *The Psycho-Analysis of Children*. London: Vintage.

Klein, M. (1997b). The Effects of Early Anxiety-Situations in the Development of the Boy. In: *The Psycho-Analysis of Children*. London: Vintage.

Lacan, J. (1958). On a Question Preliminary to any Possible Treatment of Psychosis. In: *Écrits, a selection*. Oxon: Routledge Classics, 2001.

Mendoza, S. (2001). Genital and Phallic Homosexuality. In: *Sexuality, Psychoanalytic Perspectives*, ed. Harding, C. New York: Brunner-Routledge.

Neumann, E. (1970). Mass Man and the Phenomena of Recollectivization. In: *The Origins and History of Consciousness*. New York: Bollingen Foundation.

Nunberg, H. (1935). Homosexualität, Magie und Aggression. *Internationale Zeitschrift für Psychoanalyse*, 22, 1936.

Reich, W. (1933). *The Mass Psychology of Fascism*. New York: Farrar, Straus and Giroux 1970.

Rosenfeld, H. A. (1949). Remarks on the Relation of Male Homosexuality to Paranoia, Paranoid Anxiety, and Narcissism. In: *Psychotic States, A Psychoanalytic approach*. London: Maresfield Reprints 1965.

Stoller, R. (1985). *Observing the Erotic Imagination*. New Haven and London: Yale University Press.

Thompson, C. (1950). *Psychoanalysis: Evolution and Development*. London, New Brunswick: Transaction Publishers, 2003.

Walters, P. (1965). Promiscuity in Adolescence. *American Journal of Orthopsychiatry, 35.*

Webster's Third Dictionary (1993a). Chicago: Merriam – Webster Inc. entry: promiscuity.

Webster's Third Dictionary (1993b). Chicago: Merriam – Webster Inc. entry: perverse.

Williams, C. A. (1999). *Roman Homosexuality, Ideologies of Masculinity in Classical Antiquity.* Oxford: Oxford University Press.

Willick, M. S. (1988). Dynamic Aspects of Homosexual Cruising. In: *Fantasy, Myth, and Reality, Essays in Honour of Jacob A. Arlow.* Madison, Connecticut: Internationl Universities Press.

Wittkower, E. D., Cowan, J. (1944). Some Psychological Aspects of Sexual Promiscuity. *Psychosomatic Medicine, 6.*

INDEX

Sphinx 79
symbiotic relationship
      51, 52, 58

T

taboo 5, 13, 35, 41, 46,
      49, 60, 62, 64, 68
Thebes 36, 79
"the pill" 8
transference 1, 18, 27, 32,
      33, 51, 58, 59, 60,
      62, 64, 67, 79

Z

Zeus 1, 17, 22, 23, 25, 79

Abstract

Archetypal roots of promiscuity are explored. In classical Greek and Roman mythology some promiscuous father figures may be found viz. Chronos (Saturn), and Zeus (Jupiter). Another form of Saturnian promiscuous dynamic is explored in the mythological figures of Oedipus and Antigone. This is followed by presentation of a case history. Ines is a woman in her early thirties and enters analysis because she would like to solve the recurring problem of her unsuitable partnerships, in which her partners are predominantly promiscuous. The father was psychotically disturbed and the patient was the family member who offered support to him. Psychotherapy started with stable frequency of two sessions a week. Within the transference, there appear two figures. One is that of a positive father, and the other is that of the all – knowing one. The latter may be compared with the mythological figure of Oedipus, whose intelligence was exceptional, being demonstrated in his redemption of Thebes from the Sphinx. All the same, Oedipus suffered from a promiscuously incestuous relationship with his mother Iocaste. During old age, when he was expelled, and accompanied by his faithful daughter Antigone, Oedipus was most probably psychotic. In the analysis, Ines has decided, after 200 hours of analysis, to reduce the frequency down to one session a week. The problem of analytic interpretation is described, as well as the effects of interpretation (when it finally took place) that it had on the analytic relationship and analytic process. The intimate and important link between promiscuity and incest is also explored, promiscuous actualizing the incestuous. Promiscuity is a manifest sexual activity with the unknown other. Promiscuity can also be considered as a defence against paranoia.

About the author

Matjaž Regovec is a Jungian analyst and analytical psychologist. He undertook his analytic training in Vienna while living and working in Slovenia and is a member of the London based Association of Jungian Analysts (AJA, IAAP), as well as a professional member of the Slovenian Association of Psychotherapists (ZPS).

In 1993, Matjaž founded IPAL (Institut za psihološko astrologijo in psihoanalizo Ljubljana) – Ljubljana Institute for Psychological Astrology and Psychoanalysis, of which he is still the managing director. The Institute offers a professional three-year diploma course in counselling, as well as a postgraduate training in psychoanalysis (www.ipal. si). Matjaž has a private practice in Ljubljana and works with Jungian analytic self-experiential groups in Ljubljana, Belgrade and Budapest.